WHAT YOU
SHOULD KNOW
ABOUT

PERSONNEL
MANAGEMENT

BY HOWARD FALBERG

1968
OCEANA PUBLICATIONS, INC.
DOBBS FERRY, NEW YORK

DEDICATION
TO CAROL AND OUR FIVE

Number 12 in the
BUSINESS ALMANAC SERIES

Each volume in the Business Almanac Series is designed to introduce you to an aspect of modern American Business theory and practice.

TABLE OF CONTENTS

ABOUT THE AUTHOR

Howard Falberg is a graduate of Columbia College and holds a Masters degree in Business Administration from the Columbia University Graduate School of Business.

He was Personnel Manager for a division of Continental Can Company on the west coast and thereafter served as a member of the Dean's staff at Columbia College.

Since 1965 he has been Executive Placement Director of Abraham & Straus with responsibilities in the recruitment, placement and executive development areas.

Mr. Falberg has taught courses relating to personnel subjects for Cornell's School of Industrial and Labor Relations and was an officer of the Management Development Forum.

PREFACE

I contend that the field of personnel management has more than its share of myths. A great deal of misunderstanding exists relative to the function, organization and implementation of personnel policy as a specific contributing discipline to the profitability of an organization. The following interview or variation thereof takes place hundreds of times each week at an equal number of companies.

Employer: "What aspect of our business interests you the most?"

Applicant: "Well sir, I'd like to get into personnel work."

Employer "And why is that?"

Applicant: "Because I like: A. people."

B. to work with people."

There have been occasions when I have been tempted to come back with, "so does my dog!"

While it is perfectly true that personnel management is concerned with the human resources factor in the business equation, there is a myth; half-believed by hopeful aspirants to the field, by line managers and by a number of those in the field that this staff function is a haven for "Do-gooders", whose primary concern is to help people in the social worker sense of the term. This attitude can be understood on the part of college seniors as it may reflect the altruistic idealism associated with youth. On the other hand, many line supervisors of the "old school" (which is not necessarily a function of age) are part of what I call the "mail room syndrome" and resent changing conditions and attitudes . . . e.g. "I started in the mail room working a 50 hour week at 60 cents an hour and if it was good enough for me . . ." These people resent those who, within the company, are concerned with compliance with federal and state labor laws as well as recruiting, maintaining and developing productive hourly and executive employees.

Personnel managers cannot function without the support of top management. In a supportive environment, the personnel executive can and must function (A) in a watchdog sense—providing top management with feedback relating to changes, attitudes and movements both within the company and in industry at large, (B) in an administrative sense—providing an efficient day-to-day operation and (C) in an innovative sense, relating to recruitment, management development, wage and salary administration and labor relations—thereby contributing to corporate profitability.

Performance in personnel work can be measured. Standards can and should be set for any company. Personnel work can be rewarding and stimulating to the practitioner as well as essential to a well-run profit-oriented business enterprise.

1

FUNCTIONS OF MODERN
PERSONNEL MANAGEMENT

ORGANIZATIONAL AND REPORTING RELATIONSHIPS

In viewing virtually any organization, two terms that have been used for centuries are line and staff. The former refers to elements of an organization having primary responsibility for achieving its overall objectives. In the military this would include the infantry and artillery. At industrial corporations line managers are responsible for the actual production of whatever product or service is involved. In retailing, the buyers are held accountable for profit-centered departments. Advertising executives responsible for obtaining and maintaining accounts are considered at most agencies to perform the primary functions within their organizations. Whatever the central operating function consists of within a given organization, there you will find the line organization.

A staff department is organized to aid the line in the achievement of organizational goals. While this support varies in terms of complexity and scope, it generally involves providing:

Services—such as a purchasing director, who can save a company a great deal of money

Controls—Inspection and quality control are essential to maintaining customers, not to mention the importance of internal financial control

Information and *Advice*—compliance with laws and market information through research.

When we speak of organizational relationships, however, we are not dealing with an automated computer-type process. Although in principle, staff department members provide service, counsel and support for line managers, in many instances these relationships vary in terms of responsibility and authority with the nature of the problem; strengths and weaknesses of the individuals involved, and the attitude of the man at the top.

The membership of the president's cabinet of the United States is prescribed by law. Abraham Lincoln made famous the idea of a "Kitchen Cabinet" where the counsel cf certain individuals carried much more weight than did the official department head involved.

Beyond a basic level of competence, the ability of a staff department member to function effectively depends upon his success in maintaining good working relationships with line supervisors. The quality of staff-line relationships, in many cases, accounts for the success or failure of an organization. It must be understood, however, that the integrity of the staff man must be maintained if he is not to become merely a rubber stamp or a "yes man" subject to the whims of top management and thereby lose his effectiveness.

INTERNAL COMPONENTS

While there may be a number of variations, the internal organization of a personnel department would ordinarily cover the following functions:

Employee services (cafeterias and recreation programs)
Medical (first aid and consultation services)
Communications (newspaper or magazine)
Safety, wage and salary administration, employment
Employee benefit programs (insurance, pension, savings)
Recruitment, placement, training (technical or systems)
Management development
Labor relations (grievance handling and contract negotiation)

The importance and size of each of these personnel components will vary too with the nature of a company's purpose and work force.

EVOLUTION

In many companies the personnel function was initially extracted from either a paymaster or office manager since it was seen as a record keeping procedure dealing with such matters as date of employment, jobs held within the company and wages received; occasionally background information and any disciplinary action taken. Essentially these were routine clerical tasks which certainly did not carry with them either prestige or power. Today, these original responsibilities play an important role in personnel management due to the emphasis on insurance programs, pension plans and the importance of seniority in determining eligibility for specific benefit programs and promotion.

With the advent of unionization in the 1930's, the scope and importance of personnel work assumed much greater proportions. This, plus the fact that since World War II we have been living, for the most part, in an economy that has a chronic shortage of manpower has combined to force companies as well as personnel practitioners to cast a searching eye on the objectives of the field as well as its image.

There is general agreement among responsible business leaders that the objectives of the personnel department must be the same as that of the corporation and that its general area of expertise must be the effective management of human resources. The personnel director of most large companies reports directly to the president, or to the head of a division in a multi-division corporation or to the plant manager on a local level.

Contributions to corporate goals by effectively utilizing

human resources can be measured in terms of: individual productivity, stability of the work force, long run corporate vitality, harmonious relationships, and the ability of a company to attract optimal people.

OBJECTIVE ORIENTATION

To be effective in its contributions to corporate goals, personnel's approach must be performance or objective oriented rather than task oriented, i.e. merely responding to needs both routine and extraordinary as they arise.

For instance, the approach to staffing an organization should involve determining current and future staff requirements as well as identifying and assessing current manpower skills, strengths and weaknesses. Plans can then be made and carried out which will balance input with reserves (recruitment) and output (retirements, deaths, resignations and separations). Too often the personnel department sees its responsibility merely in terms of filling requisitions.

Training, instead of a series of maintained "canned" courses plus a library of management related subjects, should stem from identifying an organization's needs in order to accomplish its objectives and then should devise programs to meet those needs.

Compensation programs must allow organizations to attract and retain optimal people. They must also be designed to reward performance, not merely seniority. There are too many companies whose programs in this area solely represent responses to demands or adjusting to one's competition.

The communications goal of personnel management is to develop effective channels which will allow managers to make proper decisions and to enable all employees to have a clear understanding of company objectives, policies and plans.

A great deal has been said and much written about what a good personnel executive should be. I have chosen thus far to emphasize what he should not be. It would become apparent to the reader if he looked at the backgrounds of a sampling of personnel managers that there is a wide variety of educational preparation and career experience. Personnel courses have recently become a fixture at most business schools and the number of personnel extension courses is almost unlimited.

The president of an organization seeking to staff a personnel department, should look first for intelligent people who have demonstrated a capacity for accomplishing things through others. Secondly, he should try to determine their understanding of what motivates people and lastly, he should look at their education and work experience as it relates specifically to personnel.

2

RECRUITING

Andrew Carnegie was supposed to have said at the height of his career that he could lose all of his plants and financial assets, but if he had his management talent intact he could recoup all of his losses within a very short period of time. A survey recently conducted by Fortune Magazine had a similar point to make. Of the top 50 corporations at the turn of the century less than 10 remain in business today. While there could be many reasons for a company's demise, failure to maintain an input of capable creative people with high potential invariably results in the inability of an organization to respond to fast changing needs of our economy. Failure to replenish company talent must inevitably result in a weakened competitive posture and lead eventually to either acquisition or extinction.

MANPOWER PLANNING

Many intelligent and currently successful organizations are asking themselves whether the market(s) they now serve will have the same kinds of needs 5, 10, and 20 years from now. If their market changes, will the skills the company currently develops in its personnel be obsolete? Can an intelligent "guesstimate" be made about objectives ten years in the future (market share, location, diversification)? Whether there will be a difference in the future or not, what kinds of skills should a firm look for now in the people coming into an organization? Are there indications today of future trends or tools that would make it wise to bring some "seed people" into the organization now? If a company is planning to expand, what kind of "lead time" does it need to provide trained, qualified people who will be ready to step into openings at the right time? Even if expansion is not anticipated, what is being done to back-stop top and middle management executives who will be retiring in the next five years?

We should recognize that there is a natural tendency for lower level managers to over rate the skills they say they require of their subordinates. In searching for inflated numbers of highly qualified people (in terms of degree level or experience), a company must face up to the danger of not providing challenge related to a man's capabilities. This contributes to high turnover during the first few years junior executives spend at a company and represents the loss of a considerable investment in these men. The cornerstone of an effective recruitment program must be manpower planning.

With its manpower objectives agreed upon, a company can then map out its strategy for effective recruiting.

MANPOWER SOURCES

A variety of manpower sources are available for a company to consider. While each source should be utilized, the relative importance of each approach will vary depending upon economic conditions, military requirements, competitive situation, etc.

Internal Search Advantages: Any company which does not attempt to identify on a regular basis the best of its non-professional or non-executive employees for possible promotion to positions of executive responsibility is doing itself and the employee a disservice. These people would definitely have an understanding of the organization which would allow them to avoid bottlenecks and to expedite the movement of goods and services which the new employee would take considerable time to learn.

Their experience on "the other side of the fence" can give them an understanding and empathy for their former co-workers. There is a certain amount of resentment towards the new college graduate who exhibits a feeling of distaste towards working with the troops as his initial assignment. This type of individual has been described as having a case of "executivitis". Some labor relations problems have resulted from this lack of sensitivity to the feelings of rank and file employees.

In our "man-poor" economy, the college graduate has demonstrated a great deal of mobility. Whether the lure is increased salary, enlarged job responsibility, better facilities or a more pleasant climate, the pirating of executives has almost become a national sport. The non-executive employee who has had a number of years with a company and has roots in the community is less likely to add to turnover figures than his college-graduate counterpart.

There can be no question that promotion from within represents the least expensive way of hiring a first line executive. One final positive factor should not be overlooked. We are supposedly living in an era which has, on the one hand, a vastly expanding economy, and on the other, signs of increasing social stratification. Promotion from the ranks can have a stimulating effect on morale, function as a safety valve for social pressure and serve as a means of motivating those with greater potential.

Disadvantages: There are disadvantages to the employer who accepts this recruiting approach as the primary one. Where this avenue to promotion is common, standards may become too low. It should go without saying that the man promoted from the ranks should be at least as capable of doing the entry level executive job as the college graduate who is straight out of school. The college graduate should not only have specialized skills but the ability to conceptualize as well. It is both unfair and unwarranted to merely assume that an unusually fine clerical or production worker has the ability to plan and direct others when his ability to perform has been judged only on the basis of his job description.

A company may be sowing seeds of discontent by promoting a non executive whom they feel will be a career first line supervisor. If this limitation is not understood (the explanation can be a very delicate matter), the employee could develop deep resentment of the "90 day wonders" who are being promoted over him because "they have a college degree". From this kind of experience, an employer may decide that all entry level executives, whether they be college graduates or promotions from the ranks must be appraised as having the same potential to reach a specific level of management (generally second or third line) before some will remain as "career" while others will continue to move upwards.

Executive Search: While many organizations have a policy of promotion from within and can maintain a pool of enough talent to match its plans for growth, they may be open to the dangers of in-breeding. There are times when a fresh approach is not only desirable but necessary. Technical skills or secrets may be proscribed from changing corporate hands and so the advantage to the acquiring employer is usually managerial skills and fresh approaches to problem solving.

On occasions when a company may be joining a bandwagon, such as introducing a Management Information Systems approach, lead time for internal development of a specialist may be non-existent. The decision may then be made to "raid" another company for an experienced executive whom they hope is dissatisfied with his present position.

Executive search or "head-hunting" firms have grown

tremendously during the last decade. Although the matter of ethics could be questioned, on occasion, these firms can provide a company with anonymity and do an effective job of screening a large sampling of people having the skills required.

A recent survey showed that the average college graduate changed jobs three times within five years of graduation. Some don't measure up to their record of high academic achievement when they enter the business world. In some cases where the transition is difficult, an employer can benefit from an individual's trial and error experience and thereby decrease his own turnover figures.

Financially, executive search has a distinct advantage over campus recruiting in that it can be initiated and terminated with virtually the same speed. Campus recruiting is a long range program where momentum is built up slowly and must be maintained.

On the other side of the coin, exorbitant salaries may have to be paid in order to persuade a man to join another organization. Since total secrecy or discretion is virtually non-existent, this may (where it involves other than top management) throw a company's salary administration program out of kilter. It may also cause current employees to question their present salaries in light of what they think they may be worth in the job market. Internal morale may be further weakened by the logical assumption that promotion from within to positions of higher management is not the company's policy.

Finally, unless some form of monopoly exists, the company that has a reputation for engaging in deliberate piracy can count on specific retaliation in kind.

Recruitment Advertising: Advertising is mistakenly seen by some as the cure-all for all non-campus recruiting. "Put an ad in the paper and your desk will be piled high with qualified responses", so they say. Most firms strike out in this effort because they fail to heed the following guide lines:

1. Use available professionals, whether they be internal advertising departments or the agency that handles the company's account. These people are familiar with the available media and should be experts with regard to size, format and copy. Just as a buyer in retailing will work with sales promotion people regarding his advertising promotions, so must personnel provide counsel in defining the specific market they wish to reach and the importance of recruiting ads regardless of their size.

2. Avoid stinginess and vague generalities — Usually the ads that are smaller than the average size for a given newspaper or magazine will draw poorly. They may reflect a myopic image of the company. Although most people at some point think of themselves as having great potential, ads which spell out "Bright Young Men" or use such hucksterisms as "Reach the Top With Us" are likely to attract the sub-standard performers of other companies. When looking for people with experience, be specific. If someone is considering a job change, he will look at those ads which describe his background, his skills, and lastly, the opportunity which may be available to him. By being specific in recruiting advertising, a degree of screening will be effected.

3. Be specific regarding replies. Indicate whether all responses will be acknowledged or only those "who meet our requirements." For the latter group, a deadline by which responders could expect to hear from the company would be a positive factor which would bolster good will.

4. Blind ads are less effective than those which list the organization. Many individuals prefer not to place their resumes in the hands of an unknown organization. The

Professional Societies

Cocktail lounges and hotel rooms do a thriving recruiting business at conventions and conferences as a complement to lectures and seminars when professional groups convene. This should not come as a shock to most companies. The best preparation a recruiting company can make is to provide a capable "constant companion" for these meetings who will develop acquaintances and contacts over an extended period of time. From his knowledge of the group plus familiarity with his company's executives, he can coordinate company efforts of whatever magnitude.

Employment Agencies—This source of recruitment is generally best for the under $12,000 salary level. For people who are reluctant to answer ads or map a job hunt strategy for themselves, agencies can cater to their needs as well as bringing them to the attention of companies who are in need of their services.

If a company is to use an agency effectively it must make certain that the agency has a clear understanding of the skill, experience and any other requirements which may be relevant to specific job needs. Otherwise the agency cannot possibly do an adequate screening job and consequently both company and agency will be wasting time and money.

COLLEGE RECRUITING

While there are a number of sources for recruiting people on a management trainee or executive level, recruiting is most closely associated with the annual pilgrimage to college placement offices by hordes of company recruiters.

College placement work is becoming more professional in terms of the calibre of men and women who enter the field. The organization and efficiency of the placement office has improved markedly. This may be due, in part, to a recognition on the part of college administrators of the importance of helping a new alumnus on the way towards his career with the hope that he will "remember" his college on at least an annual basis. A more immediate factor may have something to do with the increasing generosity of business firms towards colleges — particularly those who supply them with much needed manpower. It's fair to say that many colleges sincerely feel that they have an obligation to provide capable career counselling for their students and alumni.

Selecting the colleges to recruit at involves, in part, drawing a profile of the kind of person a company wishes to employ and matching up this profile with a number of colleges in terms of curriculum, student body academic makeup and geographic diversity of the student body. The number of colleges one recruits at would depend upon the number of trainees to be hired as well as the competition for available manpower. For example, a program of 50 campus visitations with a goal of 200 trainees is not unusual.

Once a college has been decided upon, a recruiting date must be arranged with the placement director. Although the vast majority of college seniors receive their degrees in June, the recruiting season has grown to the point where concentrated activity takes place between October and the middle of December; then a breather between the Christmas vacation and final examinations for the semester ending in January. This is followed by the final push between February and the middle of April. This calendar could change as more schools go into tri-mester plans, work-study programs or other modifications of the two semester year.

COMPETITION FOR GRADUATES

Since World War II, the United States has been described as being an "affluent society." It is also one in which the business community has experienced a chronic manpower shortage. This shortage is due, in large measure, to the necessity for maintaining a sizeable standing army.

Other areas of endeavor have increased in popularity among graduating students. Education and government have become more attractive in terms of financial rewards as well as appealing to the student's desire to contribute to the elimination of society's ills. To some extent "profit" has become a dirty word on today's campuses. These factors add up to making company college recruiting more difficult and competitive than possibly ever before.

PRE-CAMPUS VISIT PREPARATION

Prior to the campus visitation date, the personnel man responsible for the recruiting function should get as much background information as possible. He should check his internal files to see whether the company roster contains any recent graduates of the college in question. If so, he may want to utilize that person as the company representative. Such a person might have access to "decision-influencing" individuals or groups such as faculty members, student business club officers or their faculty advisors, or even fraternity presidents and team captains. With this kind of entre, information about a company can be spread in advance so as to obtain a full schedule of suitable applicants.

Some companies have created a speakers bureau consisting of executives who are not only proficient in their field but are excellent speakers as well. These executives are made available to classes and pre-professional clubs and societies. They can impart some of the personality of the company through their presentation. This will hopefully create an image of ABC Company as being an exciting place that encourages dynamic and creative people to maximize their own potential.

PRINTED MATERIAL

A number of companies choose to advertise in the college newspapers. Through this channel they hope to reach potentially interested students who might not be aware of their visit on campus. Although the consensus of opinion appears to minimize the effectiveness of campus advertising, the advantages of reaching a potential company officer who might not otherwise be aware of your visit would suggest that this technique should be used on a selective basis. If done regularly with some ingenuity, advertising can plant a good image in the minds of lower classmen and may encourage them to apply for interviews in their senior year.

Most companies that do recruit on college campuses have recruiting brochures. They vary from elaborate slick magazines which rival Life (and even Playboy) to mimeographed extensions of job data sheets. While such organizations as the College Placement Council have given some specific outlines as to what such a brochure should contain, both company and applicant alike should look for an identification of the company's current position — product(s) and market(s), its history, its plans for future growth, the training program, the functional organization of the company, and an idea of what the progress path of an individual should be like.

On campus interviews generally serve to screen people. Most placement officers provide recruiters with a resume of the students they are to see prior to the interview. This form will cover personal history, schools attended, major course of study, extra-curricular activities, jobs held, date available for employment and areas of career interest.

The interviews are usually scheduled at 30 or 20 minute intervals. Interviewers as a rule set aside the first 15 to 20 minutes in order to learn something about the applicant —how he expresses himself, what are the standards by which he judges his own successes and failures, and what brought him to the chair in which he is sitting at that moment. Since the amount of time at a campus interview is so limited, the rule of thumb most recruiters use is that the best indication of future performance lies in past accomplishments. What does the individual regard as his major achievements to date and to what extent do the activities which the applicant regards as important relate to the values and skills which the company is seeking?

Many books have been written about the art of interviewing. For the campus employment interviewer, here are a few general guidelines which may be helpful:

1. Listen to the applicant; avoid interruptions except to move the conversation to another topic.
2. Try to find out how he feels about things—about his schooling, about the jobs he has held, about his future.
3. Determine how he would react to others, and how he would respond to pressure and deadlines.
4. Look for self-confidence and assurance within the limits of reality, not as mere boasting.
5. Ask questions, but do not ask the kind that call for a yes or no answer, and do not reveal by the form of your questions what your opinions are.
6. Keep tangents from becoming the entire interview. However, it is important to find out what the applicant regards as most important to him.
7. Avoid being repetitious.

The last 10 to 15 minutes of an interview is often devoted to describing the company, its training program and the opportunities it offers to young men with ability. In other words, it's the "selling" part of the interview.

The interviewer can decide on one of several courses of action at the conclusion of the interview. Positions are generally not offered at a campus interview, but if the applicant looks particularly promising, the recruiter may invite him to the plant or office location for futher interviews. The recruiter may be uncertain whether to proceed further and will tell the applicant that he will hear from the company within 10 days. There are times when given a relaxed permissive atmosphere, both the interviewer and applicant may jointly reach the conclusion that both are looking for qualities, features and attributes which neither possess.

At the conclusion of each interview, the interviewer should record his impressions. Many companies have devised their own forms. The attached check list serves not only to record impressions but also as a guideline for areas to be covered in the interview.

Date
FROM:
Outstanding Good Fair Poor   Yes   No   **Yes   No**

TO:
RE: Interview Report of
Please evaluate the applicant on the points you have observed and place an

X in the proper column.
1. **EDUCATIONAL BACKGROUND**
      Consider: Best and least liked subjects
               Interest and ability in mathematics and statistics
2. **WORK EXPERIENCE**
      Consider: After school and vacation work
               Other paid employment

3. **APPEARANCE**
   Consider: Neatness and cleanliness
   Freedom from distracting physical characteristics
4. **POISE AND SELF-CONFIDENCE**
   Consider: Articulateness
   Mannerisms
   Emotional balance and self-control
5. **ABILITY AND INTEREST IN GETTING ALONG WELL WITH PEOPLE**
   Consider: Any job experience requiring special team work
   Participation in school activities or community affairs
   Participation in group recreation
6. **QUALITY OF THINKING**
   Consider: Logic of reasons for choice of work or for applying to us
   Powers of analysis
   Level-headedness
7. **PERSONABLENESS**
   Consider: Degree to which he engenders a feeling of pleasant enthusiasm
   Warmth and cordiality
   Likeableness
8. **MENTAL ALERTNESS**
   Consider: Quickness and directness of thinking
9. **EVIDENCE OF BEING A "HUSTLER"**
   Consider: Energy, fire and ambition
   Active aggressiveness
A. **DO YOU RECOMMEND THAT THE APPLICANT BE ACCEPTED FOR TRAINING SQUAD?**
B. **IF THE ANSWER IS "YES", FOR WHAT DIVISION?**

A company must choose and train its recruiters with a great deal of care. His negative decision regarding an applicant closes the door on any further action concerning that person. The way he impresses students is an extremely important factor in determining the image the company will have on a campus.

Students generally want to have "their day in court." They want to feel that the interviewer is interested in finding out about them and gives careful consideration to their questions as well as to their aspirations. Interviewers who take a condescending attitude towards students, who are brusque, curt and sarcastic can create an image of a company that has no respect for people. "Why bother applying for interviews if this is an indication of the treatment I can expect from them?" so the reasoning goes. There have been instances of this when it took years to re-establish a good relationship and company image.

The opposite can also hold true. Outstanding interviewers, who relate well to the students, attract top students to a company or industry that may have relatively low status.

A word of caution: the overslick "pro" who constantly employs the hard sell can be just as disastrous to a company's efforts as the rank amateur who cannot articulate nor relate to graduating seniors of today.

At the conclusion of a day's interviewing on campus, most of the capable placement directors will want to go over the results with the recruiter. He may do this in order to provide the recruiter with additional information and/or insight regarding a student. Or, he may want the benefit of the recruiter's reaction in order to do a better job of counselling the student. On a number of campuses, unfortunately, the placement director never seems to be available at the end of a day while on other campuses the placement office is woefully understaffed.

COMPANY VISITS

Company visits provide the applicant with the opportunity to meet a number of executives and to see the world of ABC Company as it may really be. This will allow a company to see a prospective employee in the environment of which he may become a part. It also enables a company to administer any tests which it feels is appropriate.

Many companies will structure their day so as to allow for multiple interviews by line managers in areas for which the applicant is being considered. A depth interview conducted by a trained member of the personnel department is often included and is most helpful although too often the pressure of sheer numbers precludes this kind of an employment guide.

As far as the applicant is concerned, surveys indicate that the most helpful part of the day consists of a period of time, usually luncheon, when he can talk to someone who was graduated perhaps a year ago and has had the same kind of job experience with the company that the applicant is being considered for. These young employees can be the best "salesmen" a company can have in this area.

Ideally, the applicant should be given a decision at the end of the day's program. If he is offered a job and does not want to give his decision that day, the usual deadline for both parties concerning a June graduate is April 1st.

SUMMER PROGRAMS

A fairly recent development is the summer program for students between their junior and senior year at college. Companies have established these programs with an eye to observing some high potential people in a work situation prior to graduation. The objective of any program of this nature is to provide early and favorable exposure to a company for students of promise. The best designed programs should involve project work under the careful supervision of a capable manager who has demonstrated his ability to develop and stimulate his subordinates. There should also be the opportunity to perform the function of a line supervisor or junior executive (filling in during vacation periods). Another essential ingredient is a series of seminars designed to give an overview of the organization using presentations by senior executives concerning their function(s) with ample opportunity for discussion.

If a company decides to embark on such a program, it must never lose sight of its objective—early and favorable exposure. There is an unfortunate tendency and a temptation to use these trainees to "fill the breech". They are often placed in a position where the work is fairly menial or routine. Turnover may have been a major problem, and supervisors have been saying . . . "if only we could get a more qualified person for that job". The positions referred to above might well have been considered entry level spots for executive trainees thirty years ago. The salary paid to these trainees is usually above that which is currently paid for the job. Companies following these practices are being short-changed in two directions. They are paying more for a given job than the market calls for and they are providing an experience not likely to encourage the trainee to return after graduation or to spread the word that this particular company is a satisfying place to work.

There is, of course, a danger in the possibility of the trainee being "oversold" or given an over-glamorized version of what to expect after graduation. One of our better known business schools has a reputation for turning out students who are supposedly ready, willing, and primed to assume a vice-president's position within a few years time. Such misconceptions lead to disillusion and waste for all concerned.

There are, obviously, jobs to be learned and understood as well as an ascending order of areas of responsibility and accountability. The crux of the matter is whether a company's environment stresses the ability to adjust to repetitive tedium in massive doses as the standard for moving upward. An intelligent organizational philosophy promotes the enlargement of job functions at all levels of management as well as an attitude which encourages suggestions for better ways of doing things.

A strong likelihood exists that not all those participating in a summer junior program will be asked to join the company upon their graduation. In cases where individuals have performed in a superior manner and there is a reasonable expectation that they wish to return the following year, a number of companies will appoint them to be "our man" or "our girl" on their particular campus. The company provides these people with information concerning the latest company developments and may bring them back to the home office for briefings during the school year. The members of these groups in turn tell the "company story" to friends and faculty members, and look for opportunities to have company representatives participate in classes, club meetings and career conferences. They may also identify campus leaders and arrange a gathering on campus so that their company personnel director may meet with this group either prior to or concurrent with their recruiting date.

A TOTAL APPROACH

A company's recruiting program should be well thought out. It must be flexible and re-evaluated regularly. Job markets change and a company must be capable of re-acting quickly.

The following check-list was compiled by The Bureau of Industrial Relations of the University of Michigan. It does an excellent job of pointing up to a company officer, either line or staff, whether his organization is getting the most mileage out of its recruiting program.

Don't
Yes No Know

Our company has written recruiting policies.

Our company conducts training programs for campus interviewers.

Efforts of recruiters from various divisions are coordinated throughout a central office.

22

We lose less than 10% of our candidates because of salary offer levels.

We know why students turn us down.

We know how much it costs to hire a college graduate.

Our starting salaries compare favorably with the going rates.

We are adapting our recruiting efforts to the new quarter and trimester systems (where applicable).

We find at least one good candidate for each 10 campus interviews we conduct.

Fifty percent of those to whom we make offers accept our offer.

We have a systematic procedure for selecting the schools we will visit.

Our recruiting brochure meets the completeness test.

The cost of our brochures is below the average cost of brochures.

The proper applicants sign up for campus interviews.

We should give gifts to placement directors.

We should visit the same schools year after year.

We follow the proper campus interviewing procedures.

Don't
Yes No Know

Information about our company reaches students before we interview them.

We schedule visits far enough in advance.

Professors are a good source of information on students' strengths and weaknesses.

Team interviewing is effective.

We have determined the best time to make an offer to a student.

All charges incurred by a student visiting our facility should be reimbursed.

We can keep a higher percentage of those we hire than the industry average.

The length of each interview we conduct is about right.

Our salary offers to recruits are not compatible with our in-company salary program.

We know how to tell if our recruiters are impressing students.

We terminate the interview the proper way.

We make use of the professional associations in the field of recruiting.

We know how to handle an overflow of applicants.

We are familiar with the training colleges give to students on how to be recruited.

We can compete successfully with other companies interviewing on campus.

As a relatively small company, we can get our share of competent, young graduates.

The trend toward the master's degree means we won't be able to hire an adequate number of bachelor's degree holders in the future.

An offer of additional training will encourage a student to accept an offer.

Our preparation for a company visit is adequate and complete.

3

COMMUNICATIONS

s we are engaged in any activity that has a
hers, we are communicating. Communication
ten, verbal or physical. A letter, a statement,
brow or a lowered voice are means we use
else to "get our message".
say and mean and exactly how we are re-
rpreted may vary. This variation or difference
uch difficulty. Each of us operates with a
lter in our mind's eye which is just as real
as the physical structure of our eye.

INFLUENCING FACTORS

number of factors which influence the way
rences. For example,
vious experiences come into play. Suppose
nvolved in an automobile accident where the
jumped the light. Your reaction to anyone
his foot on the accelerator is influenced by
nce.
sentimental attachments or loyalties which
nic, religious or geographic in nature. We
more sympathetic to those with whom we
binds than to "outsiders".
ividual has a self-concept. We try to act in
befitting the image we feel we present to
ther aspect of one's image can be seen by

A recruiter should be a technical expert
in the field for which he is recruiting.
We know how important summer job
opportunities are to recruiting success.

If nothing else, this approach should cause an individual concerned with recruiting at colleges to question whether all aspects of the problem are being considered.

College recruiting is expensive. As we noted previously, however, maintaining a healthy organization is a good deal less expensive than either a massive re-vitalization program or bankruptcy. The following survey, which was formulated by the College Relations Council, indicates the breadth of items involved.

A. 19—Recruiting Activity
1. How many new college graduates were hired from all sources?
2. How many new college graduates were hired as a direct result of college recruiting?
3. Number of recruiters you use?
4. Total number of campuses visited?
5. Number of campuses from which a recruit or recruits was hired?
6. How many campus interviews were conducted?
7. Total number of offers extended recruiting from campus interviews?

B. 19—Cost of College Recruiting
Direct Cost
1. Total cost of campus recruiting?

2. Amount spent for recruiters' travel expenses?
3. Amount spent for recruiters salaries?
4. How much was spent for candidates' travel expenses to visit the main office?
5. How much was spent for other candidate expenses such as relocation, medical examinations, and inspection or reference checks?

Indirect or Institutional Recruiting Cost
6. Amount expended for advertising?
7. Cost of brochures?
8. Expense for dues, registration, travel and living associated with membership in College Placement and other associations?
9. Cost of recruiter training?
10. Amount expended for salaries of temporary clerical employees who assist during the peak recruiting period?
11. Expense for telephone and telegraph?

Other Expenses
12. If there is any expense, direct or indirect, in your total cost of college recruiting and we have not requested it on the questionnaire, please list the expense and amount in the spaces provided below.

　　Expense:　　　　　　Amount:

Summer Program
13. If you have a summer program for students, what is the total cost of recruiting, training, salaries, administration, etc.?
14. How many students participated in your summer program?

26

our acting in a particular manner because we feel that others expect it of us. These influences vary from the humorous vignette of the overweight father playing the athlete for the benefit of his son to the member of a maligned minority group feeling no qualms about fitting a stereotype since people (the majority) have always told him that this is what he is like anyway.

4. Our perception is further modified by what our objectives are at a given point. If someone else's actions or statements run counter to what we are attempting to achieve, that fact will tend to blot out our ability to impartially evaluate what they are saying or doing.

A great deal has been said in books, articles and lectures about barriers to good communications. Possibly the greatest goal an organization can work towards is to develop an *awareness* in all employees at all levels of the results of poor communication. Such an awareness enables a manager to anticipate and eliminate potential problems. It reflects itself in an attitude which encourages an openness between supervisor and subordinate.

How many times have you heard the plaintive cry, "nobody ever tells me anything?" If a supervisor is slow in informing his group about changes or policy decisions affecting them, an index of good communications would be the extent to which they let their boss know that they feel sour and frustrated by the lack of a clear flow of information from above.

Communications consists of much more than words. As Emerson said, "What you are stands over you the while and thunders so that I cannot hear what you say to the contrary". Put in a less elegant manner, "Action speaks louder than words". The supervisor who is brusque and curt is giving his subordinates a loud and clear message that he doesn't have time to waste on them. The efficiency of the ever-present grape-vine that always provides information for people before their supervisor gets around to it, or shows him up to be withholding it bellows the message that he doesn't think they're worth bothering with. Demonstrating a thoughtful consideration of people's needs for information can go a long way in creating a climate for good communication.

The study of semantics has added a new dimension to this field. The 500 most commonly used English words have 14,000 dictionary definitions. While there are many polysyllabic words which cover a concept, they often have too many meanings which depend on the background of the hearer. Regardless of educational level, accurate "unimpressive" words do the best job of carrying a precise thought from one mind to another. Probably the best way to insure your being understood by others is to get them to "feedback" what you have said to them in their own language. Diagrams and illustrations can be very helpful in getting your message across.

Listening can be difficult, time-consuming and unproductive. It can be the key, however, to keeping channels of communications open. Listening can also be threatening to anyone. The insecure person worries—"Can I take the chance of learning something that may make me change?"

Perhaps the importance of communication makes more real sense if we accept the premise that nothing moves except through people. People are dependent upon one another. Communication channels must remain open if we are to effectively work together towards the accomplishment of goals, both individual and group.

If you will visualize an organization chart, you will see the pipelines that go downward, upward and horizontally. These are the channels of communication. When dealing with multi-levels, however, there is generally distortion somewhere along the line. Most company policies travel through many levels between the issuer and the final recipient—the person who is responsible for carrying out a directive or the individual who is affected by the policy.

Perhaps you've played the parlor game "telephone" where a number of people sit in a circle. One person whispers a statement or a story to the individual on his left and he in turn continues the process until it makes the full turn. Alteration invariably occurs along the line when each person unintentionally adds or removes certain nuances, depending on the way his perception filter operates. The end result is usually a far cry from the original message.

DOWNWARD COMMUNICATION

Distortion in downward communication generally takes two forms. A fact, learned early in business life is that within reason, an employee (at whatever level) must learn what it is his boss looks for. What is his general ranking of accomplishments? Does he stress reports, housekeeping, elimination of overtime, etc.? Some subordinates then exaggerate casual remarks into top priority projects. Witness the sad spectacle of the personnel or quality control department being turned upside down to install a program or initiate a project (where the department head had serious doubts) purely because a member of top management mentioned an article he had read or a conversation he had on the train with someone and commented, "Perhaps it might be a good idea for us."

The other approach which distorts downward communication is where a directive is issued over the strong objections of those responsible for carrying it out. In many of these instances no effort is made to either indicate top management's seriousness or gain commitment on the part of middle and lower management. Situations of this nature are great stimulants for man's gifts of ingenuity and rationalization so that while the letter of the law is obeyed, the spirit is totally lacking. If people are not committed, the implementation of a policy is doomed.

The Personal Touch. In order to improve communication effectiveness, top management will often use a variety of devices. As a means of counteracting the impersonal nature of large corporations, they attempt to recreate certain beneficial conditions which existed when the organization was small and personal contact at all levels was a way of life. This is done through personal appearances, "old-timers" nights, Christmas parties, family days, company picnics and "personal" birthday cards.

The effectiveness of this approach varies according to the organization climate which develops over a long period of time. If lower management and rank and file employees feel (with possibly good reason) distrustful of top management's motives, then these efforts will appear to be exercises in hypocrisy. The president's once-a-year Christmas handclasp smacks of sham if throughout the year he is unapproachable. If, on the other hand, this activity is one facet of a consistent effort on a year round basis to maintain open channels of communication, in all directions, one more stumbling block in the way of mutual trust and support can be removed.

House Publications. In many companies communications primarily refers to the kind of activities that public relations men are most familiar with: the company newspaper or magazine, direct mailings to employees, poster campaigns, bulletin boards, "reading-rack" magazines, pay envelope inclusions, movies, etc. In addition to births, deaths, marriages, promotions and departmental "happenings", most of these channels concern themselves with items which do not affect production and profits directly. They usually emphasize employee suggestions, new facilities, safety, customer relations, personnel policies, the company's annual statement, and so forth.

Assuming that outstanding abilities are applied to

these channels, it's worth remembering that by themselves they merely provide a one-way flow (downward) without the benefit of feedback. An intelligent management will seek to supplement these methods by providing advance information to high level supervisors before a statement or policy is given general distribution. Supervisors are often asked to supplement a general announcement by adding their own remarks to the group and encouraging questions and comments from their subordinates.

UPWARD COMMUNICATION

The most difficult condition to achieve and maintain is effective upward communication. Some say that the higher a man goes in the corporate hierarchy, the more isolated he becomes. The informality that existed on lower levels is forced to the side-lines. The widening scope of executive responsibilities and pressures generally brings about the usual barriers between the men at the top and those on or near the production line. Organizational buffers can result in a lack of information or misinformation reaching top decision-making sources. Unless subordinates feel free to provide information or suggestions which may not have even been requested, top management will lack some of the tools to intelligently evaluate and make the proper decisions.

Personnel and management literature abounds in recommendations for making people feel that they are "an important part of the team". Judging by the success of employee suggestion plans throughout the country, management finds it profitable (by statistical measure) to harness the creative ideas of employees. In addition to measuring a suggestion in terms of its profit contribution, there can be a marked improvement in morale which comes with the knowledge that the people "upstairs" will pay attention to what an employee has to say.

There is a natural tendency to tell the boss what you think he wants to hear. This results in painting a rosy picture of current operations which may be unwarranted by the facts. The supervisor who shows himself to be more concerned with placing blame on someone else's shoulders rather than being a source of help causes his people to withhold or distort information. Some of these same supervisors give the impression that requesting help from them is a sign of incapacity to do one's job. If an executive consciously heightens the fear of failure in his employees, he might just as well forget about consistent, accurate, up-to-date information from below.

In a similar vein, this same kind of executive who passes on information or directives with the attitude that it all must be self-evident usually finds himself surrounded by silent subordinates. These are people who would rather remain silent (and confused) than appear stupid or slow.

The best solution to this state of affairs is for the manager to encourage questions and comments. He should emphasize that he regards these as signs of interest and alertness — qualities that he looks for in his subordinates — and that there is no such thing as a stupid question.

A number of companies pride themselves on an "open door" policy. While the idea is a good one, its effectiveness is questionable. It's based on the concept that an employee can walk into a manager's office at any level if he feels he has a justifiable complaint. This right of appeal is most often not exercised. Understandably, the employee is concerned about going over the head of his immediate boss. The employee can reasonably anticipate his boss's reaction. There is too much risk involved and the chances of being supported are too slim.

There can be a built-in conflict between the need for supporting decisions made by supervisors and also providing an avenue for appeal beyond one's immediate supervisor. An executive can be button-holed while walking through a plant or office by an employee with a problem concerning his supervisor. The executive can refuse to listen, thereby damaging the employee's morale, or he can actively encourage complaints coming directly to him and destroy a good part of the supervisor's effectiveness. When faced with this type of problem, a reasonable solution would be to listen to the grievance and then promise to discuss it with the supervisor. By so doing, he provides a safety valve for frustration but does not cut the ground from under the supervisor. In the ensuing discussion with the supervisor, he can help talk the problem out while providing support as well. This procedure will enable a supervisor to justify or modify his decision and "save face" at the same time. Whatever final decision is reached, explanation should always come from the immediate supervisor.

EVALUATING ORGANIZATIONAL COMMUNICATIONS

The problems of horizontal communication do not involve direct lines of authority. The concern here is to achieve free exchange of information between departments. This should result in broadening the viewpoint and activities of departments which may now be isolated from each other and operating at cross-purposes.

No organization can afford to become smug about the state of its communications—both internal and external. A satisfactory condition will exist only when a constant and consistent program is maintained and supported. Canned programs are superficial and generally ineffective.

In order to periodically evaluate how well information is flowing through an organization, management utilizes attitude surveys. In all cases, maintaining the secrecy of the individual response is a cardinal rule. These questionnaires may just deal with problems in a particular area or may attempt a broad brush approach concerning feelings about one's job, conditions of work, personnel policies, supervision, etc. Answer format varies from multiple choice (alternatives) to responses indicating degree of feeling, to an open-ended approach. Findings can bring to light bottlenecks, unrecognized complaints and may result in new approaches to either work flow or prompt new supervisory training programs. This may be a means of testing the effectiveness of downward communication and eliminating some distortion in the opposite direction. The following is an example of one type of survey. (See P. 38)

As suggested earlier, formalized suggestion programs are a means of by-passing bottlenecks and provide more information about what really is happening. A study of errors can also be a powerful tool in the hands of a capable executive in determining the extent to which employees understand the rules and standards by which they are judged.

Many companies provide checklists for its managers as guide lines for the self-audit of communication program effectiveness. The following is a composite form:

	Present Practice	
	Is Adequate	Needs Attention

I. Downward Communication

Frequent meetings are held on plans and policies, goals and objectives, changes in schedules or operations. Discussion participation is encouraged.	( )	( )

Information is passed along promptly to all department members at the same time. Briefing takes place prior to the act. ( ) ( )

Decisions are passed along immemediately so that they are not garbled by the grapevine. ( ) ( )

When information is given to the press, employees receive it first. ( ) ( )

Employees are always briefed re: new assignments by supervisors. ( ) ( )

After giving instructions; comments, questions and opinions are elicited and listened to. ( ) ( )

II. Upward Communication

Policy meetings are held with all concerned. Scheduling is announced in advance to invite participation and (where appropriate) recommendations. ( ) ( )

When opinions are expressed counter to a management proposal, they are treated as sincerely and constructively meant. ( ) ( )

Ideas and suggestions are encouraged and given careful consideration. ( ) ( )

III. Horizontal Communication

Inter-departmental contacts via visits, meetings and consultations are held to pool new approaches and better methods that may exist elsewhere. ( ) ( )

JOB ATTITUDE SURVEYS   (For Table 2)

A wide variety of factors influence the satisfaction one gets from one's work. Twenty such conditions have been included in this Job Attitude Survey. For each question, would you check the number which indicates **how important** a given factor is to you, **personally**. Please check one number in the left column. Would you also check the number which indicates the extent to which you are **personally** satisfied with each factor.

HOW IMPORTANT TO YOU IS:

1. Doing work which is interesting and challenging?
1. Of great importance
2. Of considerable importance
3. Somewhat important
4. Not important
5. Does not apply

3. Having a position which makes full use of your abilities?
1. Of great importance
2. Of considerable importance
3. Somewhat important
4. Not important
5. Does not apply

5. Having a good idea of just what is expected of you on your job?
1. Of great importance
2. Of considerable importance
3. Somewhat important
4. Not important
5. Does not apply

7. Having steady employment in this company?
1. Of great importance
2. Of considerable importance
3. Somewhat important
4. Not important
5. Does not apply

HOW SATISFIED ARE YOU WITH:

2. The nature and challenge of the work you are now doing?
1. I'm well satisfied
2. I'm satisfied
3. I'm not satisfied
4. I'm quite dissatisfied
5. Does not apply

4. The extent to which your current position makes full use of your abilities?
1. I'm well satisfied
2. I'm satisfied
3. I'm not satisfied
4. I'm quite dissatisfied
5. Does not apply

6. The knowledge you have of what is expected of you on your job?
1. I'm well satisfied
2. I'm satisfied
3. I'm not satisfied
4. I'm quite dissatisfied
5. Does not apply

6. The likelihood that you will have steady employment in this company?
1. I'm well satisfied
2. I'm satisfied
3. I'm not satisfied
4. I'm quite dissatisfied
5. Does not apply

If you were **not satisfied** with the factors listed below—
1. Please state briefly the reason for your answer, and/or, 2. Please state briefly any suggestions for corrections or improvements.
   If you were **satisfied** with the factors listed below—feel free to make any comments or suggestions you wish.

4

ORIENTATION AND PLACEMENT

When a man begins a new job, his motivation is usually at or near its highest point while his productivity is generally at the other end of the scale. A major organization objective is to raise the individual's productivity while maintaining his motivation at its initally high level.

Just as a child's personality is molded during his first few years, so can an individual's attitude towards his employer be shaped by his experience during the first few days or weeks on a new job. The orientation period offers great potential for high motivation. There are companies which spend a great deal of time and money in recruiting high-potential men and women and then literally squanders these efforts by handling his or her orientation in a sloppy manner.

Poor efforts in this area don't generally reflect indifference, but rather the way management recognizes its priorities. Those executives who feel "under the gun" every day may not have the time to do a complete job or feel that top management does not regard this activity as important. Others plainly fail to understand the uncertainty and concern a new man has.

INITIAL INFORMATION

There are two kinds of information which concern the new employee. The first and most immediate areas include:

1. Meeting fellow employees in his work area.
2. Being shown "vital areas" — cafeteria, rest rooms, medical office.
3. Learning work regulations — hours of work, lunchtime, overtime.

4. Knowing about sick leave, holidays, and vacations.
5. Understanding salary arrangements—where he is paid, when he is paid, how he is paid (cash or check), deductions.
6. Understanding probationary period—length, follow-up.
7. Knowing what to do if he is to be absent.
8. Obtaining an explanation of his department's organization and his specific role in it.
9. Knowing what to do in case of an accident on the job.
10. Learning about discounts for the purchase of company products and other employee perquisites.
11. Knowing about salary reviews or any built-in increments during his orientation and/or training period.

If orientation planning is poor or there is no planning at all, an employer-employee relationship can easily lead to misunderstandings. This in turn can lead to frustration, apathy and eventually turnover. Where early attrition or excessive turnover can be traced to this cause, management should be charged with wasteful negligence. Most medium to large sized corporations spend an average of $10,000 on each executive trainee during his first year on the job. Inefficiency in this area is quite costly. The second area of great concern during this period is the matter of expectations—the trainee's and the company's. Most people begin their career concerned with such questions as:

* Is this the area of work I can do best?
* Will I have opportunities to learn and grow?
* Can I be creative here?
* Will I be given real responsibility?
* Will I be able to use some of the tools and principles learned at school?
* Will I be recognized for what I achieve?
* Can I maintain my integrity and individuality?

40

MANAGEMENT ATTITUDES

Many executives, on the other hand, have somewhat of a jaundiced view of the new employee. They view the "bright young man" with suspicion and their thinking is based upon a number of premises:

* The recent college graduate has an inflated opinion of his worth and an unrealistic timetable for advancement.
* The recent college graduate is too theoretical and naive to be able to effectively deal with people.
* The recent college graduate is too immature and inexperienced to be given initial responsibility.
* The recent college graduate may have potential, but he needs practical experience, lots of it, before he can be trusted to make any decisions.
* The recent college graduate is too concerned with fringe benefits and retirement.

These and a host of other similar opinions point to the likelihood of friction during a new employee's orientation period. The tokens of success for one generation are generally not the same as those which their sons and daughters will hold. This "generation gap" and disparity of expectations is usually bridged, however, by the experiences which come from working together.

Realizing that these orientation problems exist is a strong argument for an organization to place responsibility for initial training completely in the hands of the personnel department. This would also mean that trainees salaries should be part of the personnel department's budget so that they may be placed in situations where the supervisor has demonstrated abilities to develop new people.

In cases where trainees are being used solely as a highly paid "pair of hands", the personnel department should have the right to remove and place them in a learning situation. Most trainees do not object to menial

work if they are shown where their work fits into the
total picture; that their efforts are contributing to the
achievement of departmental goals; and that it is part of
the development process.

To be sure, it is the trainee who must adjust to the
organization. The strains which may be involved in this
adjustment can be minimized, however, by understanding
the causes and making a real effort to treat high potential
people on an individual basis.

TRAINING PROGRAMS

The idea of formalized corporate training programs
first took hold during World War II when it became
necessary to train huge segments of the population for
positions in heavy industry. Assembly lines had to be
tended by people without industrial experience and jobs
were therefore broken down to the simplest components.
In 1946 and thereafter the same approach was applied to
management training programs. The emphasis was on
long formalized programs with a great deal of job rotation
and classroom lectures which spoon-fed material on an
elementary level to large groups of college trained people.
It seems that force-feeding minutia was the order of that
day.

Another approach, which has a longer history, is the
"sink or swim" method. In some circles this is called "on
the job training". While this technique certainly provides
early involvement, it can also be very inefficient and fail
to motivate the junior executive by completely restricting
him to a narrow view of the company.

Findings indicate that 90 per cent of an individual's
learning results from his day to day relationship with his
supervisor and peers. The other 10 per cent comes from
formalized training.

42

At this point we are concerned with the type of training program that serves to orient the new employee to his job and to the company. The most effective of these programs emphasize the supervisor-subordinate working relationship as well as the individual's needs. These programs also take the view that a great deal of initial job rotation does not work. The "grand tour" trainee is forced to spend a great deal of time in observation and "make-work" activities which are neither stimulating to the individual nor productive for the organization.

PLACEMENT

In its general sense, placement should insure having the right man for the right job, in an area where he can make maximum use of his talents—thereby maximizing his contribution to organizational objectives. This also means seeing to it that the high-potential employee has challenge and diversity in his assignments. Too many people list as the reason for a job change, "I felt I was getting into a rut" or "I felt shelved and forgotten" or "I didn't feel a sense of participation". From the company's standpoint, effective placement means getting the greatest return on a costly investment.

As an individual goes beyond his initial assignment someone in the organization should be responsible for making certain that assignments involve skill development and fulfill personal as well as company needs. In this way the organization will have a maximum number of highly qualified candidates for positions at middle and upper levels of management as these jobs become available. An organization which does not audit its manpower skills nor carefully plan the growth of its executives to make them more versatile often has to search outside the company at great expense in order to fill many of its openings.

Since the goal of effective placement must be the maximum development of a company's human resources, some of the means towards this end are: replacement charts, promotion lists, rotational assignments, "off-site" workshops and seminars as well as "in-plant" programs.

Recognition of an individual's developmental needs can best be found in appraisal analyses. By identifying areas of strength and weakness, specific development recommendations can be made for the individual. If this approach is to be effective, however, the supervisor's appraisal must deal with performance related to goals and objectives rather than to character traits.

INEFFECTIVE PERFORMERS

When discussing input, a personnel manager remarked, "if I batted 1.000, I'd be worth one million". Every organization has a number of people who are rated by their supervisors as sub-standard performers. This comes about despite careful concern for selection, placement and development. Among the most common causes for ineffective performance are:

Obsolescence—Man's knowledge of science and technology has increased at a phenomenal rate. The information a young engineering graduate took from his Alma Mater five years ago may, in large measure, be obsolete today. Computerization has caused radical changes in production and financial control techniques.

Some people are constantly "retooling" themselves and stay on top of new developments. Others either for personal or environmental reasons fall to the point where they cannot or will not catch up.

Overpromotion—Assessments can be wrong and people can push for or be pushed into positions which require skills and/or experience they lack. On occasion, the demands of the job are above the individual's potential. *Loss of Motivation*—When an individual feels frustrated or thwarted in achieving his career goals he will often look for other avenues of satisfaction off the job. His performance then becomes perfunctory and his attitude passive. He sees himself as "serving out his time".

More often than not, an employee's performance is evaluated subjectively. As a result, the line between the effective and the ineffective performer is difficult to define. The easy way out is too often taken—demotion or involuntary separation. How many managers, new to their position, find themselves inheriting a "problem" and are told to be the "hatchet-man"?

Yes, it is difficult and time consuming to attempt to instill the enthusiasm in an employee who has not felt it for some time. Yes, it is difficult to help re-train a once valuable technician. Yes, it is difficult to upgrade employees who have been static for some time and passed over for promotion. If the effort is not made, however, the future losses to both company and economy will be atronomical. The changes (automation and sophisticated management information systems) which are now taking place in industry will intensify in the future. A constructive effort to salvage skills is far less costly than a constant external talent search.

A Constructive Approach

Elements of a constructive approach include:
1. An effort should be made early in the career of each employee to identify areas where there is need for improvement.
2. The employee should be appraised regularly by his supervisor and his evaluation discussions should be based on his performance vis-a-vis agreed upon goals and objectives.

3. Outside courses (university, professional or consulting groups) and in-plant training programs should be used where appropriate, recognizing that 10% of what the individual learns will be learned through formal programs.

4. Changing the environment or the supervisor can occasionally result in "miraculous" improvements. The "bum" in situation A can become the "hero" in situation B. Changing assignments may result in utilizing skills which were heretofore unknown.

Releasing a person for sub-standard performance may be the proper solution for both company and individual. There is often a great deal of truth in the manager's comment, "We think that you can make better use of your talents elsewhere." It is inexcusable however, when an employee gets his first inkling of poor performance at the time he is released. This is especially so in the case of long-term employees.

EVALUATING ORIENTATION AND
PLACEMENT EFFORTS

Since most turnover in a company takes place during the first few years of an individual's employment, there are a number of ways of identifying trouble spots:

1. Are we losing desirable people in particular departments, locations, or kinds of jobs?

2. Is there a discernible pattern in the people we are losing? i.e. age, sex, education, experience.

3. Is there a relationship between those people we lose and their evaluations or appraisals? Are we losing our "mistakes" or our high-potential performers?

4. Do our historical data agree with the above findings? Have there been significant changes?

EXIT INTERVIEWS

A further means of evaluating a company's efforts in this area is the *Exit* interview. It is generally best to use a skilled interviewer for this task. The purpose of these interviews is to get an honest reason for the termination (particularly if it is voluntary) and to get feedback which may enable a company to improve its efforts with people as well as auditing its organization's effectiveness. Among the areas to cover are:

1. What are the real reasons for the individuals leaving the company?

2. What could the company have done to prevent his leaving? Where did the company fall down?

3. If he is going to a new job, how does it compare with his current situation—salary, type of work, conditions?

4. Are there problem areas affecting morale which the company may be unaware of? Can he be specific?

5. What are his feelings towards the company? Is it as favorable as possible?

FOLLOW-UP QUESTIONNAIRES

Some companies feel that there is too much emotionalism at the time of separation and therefore use a questionnaire which they send to former employees three or six months after they leave. Multiple choice questions are most commonly used. Included among these might be:

a. Was your work hampered by lack of equipment, supplies or support people?

My work was hampered: (check only one answer)

    ( ) Very seriously

    ( ) Considerably

     ( ) Moderately
     ( ) Slightly
     ( ) Not at all

b. Did you feel that pressures upon you were out of proportion to the rewards of the job?

  The pressures were:

     ( ) Always out of proportion
     ( ) Usually out of proportion
     ( ) Half of the time out of proportion
     ( ) Rarely out of proportion
     ( ) Never out of proportion

c. Did your supervisor delegate responsibility to you?

     ( ) No attempts were made to delegate responsibility
     ( ) Attempts were rarely made
     ( ) Occasionally responsibility was delegated
     ( ) Usually responsibility was delegated
     ( ) Responsibilities were always delegated to me.

d. Did you feel that your supervisor demonstrated an active and helpful interest in your training and development?

  My supervisor:

     ( ) Never demonstrated an active interest
     ( ) Rarely demonstrated an active interest
     ( ) Occasionally demonstrated an active interest
     ( ) Usually demonstrated an active interest
     ( ) Always demonstrated an active interest

e. Was there a way for you to find out whether your work was improving so that you could tell what progress you were making?

     ( ) There was no way to find out
     ( ) It was very difficult to find out
     ( ) There was a fair way to find out
     ( ) There was a good way
     ( ) There was an excellent way

f. How would you compare the rate of pay of your

present job with rate of pay of your job at ABC Company?

My present pay is:

( ) Considerably higher

( ) Somewhat higher

( ) Same

( ) Somewhat less

( ) Considerably less

g. What was the primary reason that caused you to leave ABC?

h. What features attracted you to your present job?

Summary

The first year of an individual's employment with a company can be the most decisive. Patterns of behavior, performance, and attitudes are often molded during this period of time. Foundations are laid for both job satisfaction and level of motivation. The organization must strive to orient the individual and start him on his career in such a manner that he can see himself growing, developing and utilizing his skills to maximum advantage for himself and the company for which he works.

5

MANAGEMENT DEVELOPMENT

Unlike new equipment, like automatic elevators, which has standard specifications and is installed by one department, management development programs can only be installed by having commitment from top management on down. Management development is a *line* function. It can't be done by Personnel, although Personnel may design and monitor the program, and measure how it's going as well as suggest revisions. While the personnel department is vital therefore, to the development, maintenance and continuance of most of these programs, lack of management commitment condemns any such activity to failure before it begins.

Antagonism towards these programs by line managers could reflect a lack of understanding or indifference to several elements of "managing". We should certainly agree that the development of subordinates and the planning, control, and evaluation of their work are major managing activities.

Whether formal programs exist or not, some managers will perform these development activities in an outstanding manner; others will perform less satisfactorily, while a few will not manage at all in these areas. No organization, however, with hopes of survival, can afford to leave these activities to chance.

Behavioral scientists have been active since the 1930's attempting to learn more about the dynamics of the working group. They have been studying organizations in order to learn how human beings function within them. Their findings have been aimed at improving the effectiveness of the individual and the group or company of which he is a part. In a recent article, the senior editor of Fortune Magazine stated, "What industrialization was to the 19th century, management is to the 20th century".

We have been emphasizing that while techniques and devices are important, they are merely tools which may be used within the context of an environment. It's easy enough to issue memoranda or declare a policy, but this does not necessarily change behavior. What is even more difficult, however, is to change people's attitudes.

Perhaps ancient Greek civilization presents the best examples of extremes in terms of placing value on the individual. The Athenian climate encouraged a great degree of involvement and concern for the individual. The Spartan climate represented the other end of the continuum in that they had great task orientation. When compared to group goals, individual needs were meaningless.

In our industrial society, the counterparts could be what is called "participative management" on the one hand and authoritarian leadership on the other.

A FORECAST

In one form or another, as we have earlier said, one of the most constant elements in our society is change. New cycles occur with increasing rapidity and we are now witnessing a number of powerful changes in the attitudes of those who are entering the job market.

As the life expectancy of the individual increases, so will the length of his working career. While the "under 25" segment of our population is increasing, so is the "over 65". In spite of shorter work weeks and early retiremment, we see an increase in "moonlighting" and the beginning of new careers at the conclusion of the old.

We live in a highly mobile society. Each year twenty percent of the American population moves. Many of the factors which formerly contributed to the stability of a work force such as ties to a community, family group or company have been downgraded. This has been due in part to a growing commitment to one's profession rather than loyalty to a business firm, as well as the ease of long range transportation and communication. We see this not only in the business world where a number of specialists voluntarily leave their job each year in order to work with leading professionals in their field but in academic circles too.

We are also beginning to see a lessening of organization patterns based upon authority due to one's "rank". The new emphasis places responsibility on the shoulders of those who have the know-how to guide projects to their successful completion. Jobs are becoming less structured and creativity is elicited rather than assigned. A manager will find himself playing a number of roles—manager, innovator, resource person or expeditor; depending upon the project and the skills he offers.

The concept of continuing education will demonstrate its validity with great urgency in the years to come. More people will become concerned with obsolescence and there will be a proliferation of university courses, trade association courses and correspondence courses.

A RATIONAL APPROACH

What principles should we use as guidelines in determining a rational approach to management development? The individuals comprising an organization should be so motivated that their behavior enables the organization to achieve its objectives while providing people with meaningful rewards and personal satisfaction.

Some basic definitions are important. By *motivation* we mean the result of the interaction between an individual and his goals—*why* a person behaves in a particular manner.

Behavior is the function of a person in a given situation.

A person is the sum total of his interests, abilities and attitudes.

A situation is organizational values and leadership.

A good manager creates conditions where people feel they are working for themselves. By and large we have failed to *make people perform* in a large organization as we would like them to. One of the gauges of a manager's effectiveness is his ability to create opportunities for people to develop and grow.

INTEGRATED EFFORT

Management development activities should represent an integrated, company-wide effort. The areas for attention should be the company environment, formalized programs, work concept and the way the organization views the role of the supervisor.

Environment

1. What is the company's economic position? Is it expanding so that employees can look forward in confidence not only to holding their jobs but to increased job opportunities?

2. How is the company organized? Does most decision-making come directly from the top with little authority passed on? As a rule, decentralization emphasizes individual freedom, responsibility and accountability. Increasing self control and self direction generally heightens a sense of "ownership" in a work force.

3. Are people encouraged to be creative? In most companies people are often ridiculed for new ideas. This too often results in deadly conformity.

4. Does management realize that it is *always* communicating but that most of the time it is not managing this process well? We seem to encourage cumbersome paperwork in the name of communication action. The closer the formal and informal lines of communication are, the stronger the actual communication will be.

5. Does the organization foster status consciousness? Jobs should be described in terms of function rather than status symbols. The flaunting of status difference merely serves to separate people within the same organization. It certainly does not maximize collaborative efforts.

6. Are people encouraged to displace themselves through promotion? This can be a prime motivator towards the stabilization of a work force.

FORMALIZED PROGRAMS

Planning Meetings √

The concept and process of management by objectives will be covered in the next chapter. At this juncture we are pointing up the need for periodically determining goals and objectives for the coming six months or a year as well as outlining the means for achieving them. These goal-setting meetings between the *individual and his boss,* not top management or Personnel are supplemented by performance review sessions which cover achievements, six-month and long-range goals.

Educational Assistance

These programs generally involve tuition refunds. They may be applicable to degree granting programs or extension courses. The refunds vary from 50 to 100% or may be on a sliding scale, depending upon grade received.

Compensation

The approach here must be based as much as possible on merit. It should be a function of the individual's contribution to the organization.

Attitude Surveys

Every management should try to get as much feedback as possible from all of its employees. Productivity can be affected in a very positive way by inviting ideas and suggestions in areas that might formerly have been considered management prerogatives.

Work Simplification √

In order to harness the ingenuity of employees, they should be given this kind of training which may enable them to function in problem solving areas. Without an understanding of methods improvement techniques, they might be incapable of channeling their ideas.

CONCEPT OF MEANINGFUL WORK

A person will generally apply his greatest efforts in situations where he has a voice involving three basic areas:

Planning—The concern here is with problem solving and goal setting—being able to influence the use of materials and manpower.

Doing—Can the individual implement the plan? Can he see it through to its conclusion?

Controlling—This is an on-going process. Can he measure, evaluate and correct circumstances as they occur and revise plans as measurements indicate need?

All meaningful work consists of all of these management functions. The effective manager must be involved in all these elements of work.

ROLE OF THE SUPERVISOR

The effective supervisor attempts to create an open problem solving climate. He strives to build trust between people and groups. He can achieve this by:

1. Participating with subordinates in problem solving and goal setting.
2. Creating situations for learning to occur naturally.
3. Enabling people to check their own performance.
4. Providing a climate in which people have a sense of working for themselves.

In performing this role he functions best by:

1. Giving visability to company goals.
2. Providing budgets and facilities.
3. Mediating conflicts.
4. Staying out of the way to let people manage themselves.

SOME CURRENT DEVICES

There are a number of management development devices which are currently receiving widespread acceptance. The three listed below are all concerned with the development of interpersonal skills.

Business Games

This involves simulating a "real life" business situation with the participants playing assigned roles. Role playing is pre-arranged to include elements of both problem solving and conflict. At the end of a session, the group analyzes what took place (otherwise known as *process*). This discussion concerns how people relate to each other, how they interact and what kind of feelings were generated.

T Groups

It is designed to make people more sensitive to themsleves and others. The setting for these meetings is always removed from work locations and is generally somewhere out in the country where the group can be isolated. The T group consists of a dozen or so people and one or two leaders. There is no formal agenda and the group feeds upon, grows, and gains insights from their interaction with each other. The emphasis is on process and the individual is forced to re-examine his self-concept, his behavior, and his attitudes towards others.

Managerial Grid

Robert R. Blake and Jane S. Mouton devised a method of assessing managerial styles. They felt that the two primary variables which influences a manager are his concern for production and his concern for people. The two axes are scaled from one (minimum) to nine (maximum). The horizontal axis represents production and the vertical represents people. The ultimate is a manager who realistically scores nine, nine. Blake and Mouton have developed long range workshop programs which concentrate on managerial style, group effectiveness efforts, goal setting and implementing established gains.

6

MANAGEMENT BY OBJECTIVES

Incentives in industry are generally related to progress toward goals—sales, production, profit. Most of management development in the past has not been related to this due to problems of measurement. As if by response to this form of criticism, management by objectives (or by results) has become the most popular and exciting new management technique, certainly in this decade. It is a quantifiable method of relating much of the motivational research to date with objective measures of evaluating performance. Management by objectives brings the focus of the organization back to the activities and accomplishments of the individual.

SOME DEFINITIONS

In order to put this area in the proper perspective, let us agree on three definitions:

Objectives—conditions to be achieved and sustained for an organization to be successful.

Goals—end results to be achieved within a given period of time.

Plans—actions taken as a means of achieving a goal.

BROAD OUTLINE

The technique involved is relatively simple and certain approaches have been in use for some time—with some very basic differences. The process involves:

1. Each executive draws up a list of his objectives, goals

and plans for the coming period. They should be prepared in light of where and how the individual feels he can contribute to the overall objectives of the organization. These objectives should be stated, wherever possible, in measurable terms such as dollars, percentages and amounts. Unless a completely new man is involved, each executive must first be allowed to draw up his own targets. If we wish to gain commitment on the part of each employee to his goals and objectives, it becomes self-defeating to have the boss approach the subordinate initially with "these are your goals and objectives".

2. The employee and his boss discuss the targets which the employee has drawn up. The boss brings to this discussion broader information concerning company plans as well as his own ideas about what he will discuss with his own manager. He also brings his ideas about his subordinate's strengths, weaknesses and developmental needs. The employee, in turn, knows his job, has some ideas concerning his abilities and the direction he wishes his career to take. The two men must agree upon goals which are challenging yet attainable. Both men must be committed to their accomplishment.

3. Each manager sets about to put his plan into action and accomplish the goals and objectives he agreed to reach.

4. At the end of the agreed-upon period of time, accomplishments are reviewed in terms of the goals which were set. The discussion between supervisor and subordinate covers achievements, areas where performance fell short of the goal, and problem area which require action on either man's part. Unrealistic goals or organizational difficulties can be dealt with. With this discussion as a base, the process repeats itself for the next period of time.

The employee who is involved in management by objectives is more thoroughly committed to the total management process. He has helped to plan most of his work. Within the confines of those plans he has decision-making authority.

As a point of view, this approach gets people to think in terms of results, not activities. Thus accountability goes hand in hand with authority. In order not to squelch the person who is being given responsibility for the first time in a particular area, an allowance should be made for a degree of error.

LINE-STAFF CONFLICT

Whether a man be in a line or a staff department, his position and department must be justified in terms of its contribution to organization objectives. Staff departments generally require experts in their particular field. As a rule, the decisions of a staff man should be maintained within his area of authority.

A degree of conflict between line and staff is inevitable, but its extent can be lessened if the staff department is not viewed as "advisor" or "consultant" but rather as an equal partner having measurable areas of responsibility and accountability.

FORMAL APPRAISALS

Programs of formal appraisal or performance evaluation have been in existence for some time. The emphasis, unfortunately, has been on characteristics or traits—a subjective approach by the supervisor rather than results oriented. To a large extent the supervisor was playing God and psychiatrist rolled into one. Quite often there would be a difference of opinion between supervisor and subordinate on matters irrelevant to performance and the discussion became completely unsatisfactory. The supervisor would feel that he could not communicate with the subordinate and the subordinate would become disturbed with his boss for passing unwarranted value judgments concerning his character.

Consider the supervisor who stated that his assistant did not "exude an aura of leadership". To say that this was a vague comment which invited countless interpretations would be an understatement indeed. Then there was the manager who complained of his assistant's lack of dedication. By itself this statement might imply a relationship between "dedication" and the number of beads of perspiration on the assistant's brow.

This kind of vagueness eliminated a great deal of appraisal program effectiveness. Discussions did not involve whether goals were achieved, and if not, what problems were involved. Coaching and counseling under management by objectives becomes related to better ways of getting the job done through *managing*—directing the attainment of objectives.

PROBLEM AREAS

Priorities

If all goals are not specifically included or related, some are sacrificed because of a degree of conflict concerning ranking or importance. This requires resolving in advance such questions as sales volume versus profitability, or cost-reduction versus adequate maintenance.

Flexibility

Business conditions change and managers must have the flexibility to revise or modify their goals. Rigidity in this area could be disastrous.

Reasonable Goals

Agreed upon goals must be challenging and encourage the manager to "stretch" his capabilities. If goal setting mettings turn into bargaining sessions, however, an element of hedging and dishonesty will enter the picture and may lead to complacency. Unattainable goals lead to apathy.

Company-Wide Integration

If management by objectives is to succeed, goals must be set at all levels of management and they must be in harmony with company-wide objectives. Too often, departments work in isolation. If the program only relates to an individual's annual appraisal session, the organization is not reaping value to the extent that it should.

Management by objectives is a total approach to managing. It involves the participation and commitment of all managers to the company's success. It also points up the fact that company success depends upon the achievement of individual goals.

ESSENTIAL FACTORS FOR SUCCESS

A number of factors, in consonance with each other are necessary for success. These are:

1. *Job understanding* (supervisor-subordinate)—This should be mutually arrived at. The subordinate has the burden of expressing what he thinks his job is. There should always be an effort to build the job around a person's abilities. The supervisor should also ask his subordinate, "What would you like to do?"

2. *Set Objectives*—The individual sets goals for himself under the umbrella of department goals. Elements of goal objectives include:
    a. Time factor
    b. Quantitative factor
    c. Allowance for change and adjustment
3. *Basis for Evaluation*—Annual reviews alone don't work. Quarterly reviews seem to work best. Frequent reviews offer opportunities to coach and counsel. The individual doing the counseling should be close to his subordinate's work.
4. *Ongoing Discussions*—The boss is out of a role where he is playing God. He is seen more as a source of help. This lends itself to holding more problem-solving discussions.
5. *Performance and Salary Reviews*—Some believe in separating the two discussions. An individual will not respond to performance appraisal when his chief concern is dollars; most companies, however, do believe in relating performance to compensation.
6. *Supportive Group Activities*—Departmental sharing causes greater inter-departmental cooperation. Knowing what others are doing helps achievement of both individual and departmental objectives. Inviting outside staff people can be helpful and provide other perspectives.
7. *Manager-Subordinate Relationship*—If management by objectives is to be successful, there *must* be mutual trust, openness and frankness. Leveling is essential.

All seven factors must be involved for total success. Surveys indicate that success is also related to programs that are tailored to a plant, a division, a department—not the total corporation.

7

COMPENSATION

A variety of factors affect the climate of an organization and the motivation of the individual. It would be ostrich-like if we neglected the proverbial "root"—money.

Compensation should be viewed as a total package having three primary components: base pay, indirect pay that has tangible value, and employee perquisites.

A. Base pay consists of a specific amount of money which an employee is guaranteed on a regular basis for services, duties or responsibilities performed.

B. Indirect compensation includes those items generally referred to as fringe benefits. According to the United States Chamber of Commerce, fringe benefits cost American employers an average of 26 percent of payroll. These items range from retirement programs to stock options to tuition refunds, savings plans, and bonuses, to mention a few. A category could also be included for pay received for time not worked. This would cover payment while on jury duty or serving in the military reserve; holiday and vacation pay.

C. Perquisites can involve employee discounts on company products or a company car; items which can be costed out. On the other hand, there are items which have psychic or ego-related value such as office decor, *two* secretaries, and the famous (or infamous) key to the executive washroom.

By virtue of being part of an organization, an individual may also benefit from recreational facilities, discount travel tours, credit unions, discount tickets to theatrical or sporting events. These advantages are enjoyed by all, regardless of performance or output. Benefits of this nature are promoted in the interests of morale or employee health. Outside of generating a feeling that this makes XYZ "a good place to work", it is difficult if not impossible to measure their motivating influence.

COMPENSATION PHILOSOPHY

An effectively run corporation must develop a pay philosophy which is both consistent and allows the company to maintain the initiative rather than always responding to competitors and/or market circumstances. As is the case with other aspects of personnel management, top-line executives must be committed to compensation philosophy implementation if it is to achieve its objectives.

Policy statements such as, "we will pay salaries in our company at least equal to, or better than pay for comparable positions in the area or industry" may not mean very much. Let us assume that all companies adopt this approach. Who then would be below the average? Implementing this "keeping up with the Joneses" approach involves taking or participating in an annual wage and salary survey for a city, area or industry. If a company is at or above the average, all is considered well. Occasionally when a survey does not prove a pre-determined point, the solution is to take another survey.

Objectives

The objectives of a well conceived compensation program should be:
1. To attract and obtain optimal employees (quantity and quality).
2. To retain competent and promotable employees.

3. To motivate employees towards maximum performance.
4. To remain competitive and protective of the stockholders' interest.

COMPANY IMAGE

Several companies and industries develop a reputation with regard to pay pattern. Banks and utility companies, for example, have a reputation for low pay and high security. Defense oriented industries, on the other hand, are categorized as feast or famine operations. When the going is good, the pay is high.

Some companies fall into these compensation stereotype traps and find themselves limited in the personnel they can obtain. Once a company decides on the kind of people it wants, its compensation philosophy and practice should be geared towards achieving this objective. It should also go without saying that once this philosophy is developed, it should be zealously and continuously *communicated.* If a long standing company policy is changed, that should be stressed too.

FRAMEWORK

When compensation is viewed by employees as being fair, it will serve, as a rule, to ward off those who would tempt employees with an offer of a modest salary increase. Conversely, when a company's basic wage and salary structure is regarded as non-competitive or inequitable, employees will tend to take the maximum advantage of any and all benefits and experience. They will consider themselves in a temporary situation, and actively make themselves available on the job market.

CHARACTERISTICS OF MONEY

1. It is universal and a point of comparison on a widely understood and accepted basis.
2. It is a symbol which is a means of demonstrating whatever values the individual considers important —achievement, power, security.
3. It can help satisfy human needs at all levels— physiological, security, esteem and recognition.

Money varies in importance to the individual, depending upon his economic status and his goals at a given point. To what extent, in other words, does money make the achievement of an individual's financial and non-financial goals possible? Recognizing the nature of money as a motivator, company policy should emphasize:

A competitive and equitable wage and salary structure. Employees should not have a basis for feeling that they are being "used" or that the organization is taking advantage of them. The fact that a company's wage and salary administration may be based on the latest job description or job-evaluation plans and techniques has little meaning if employees feel it to be inequitable.

All things being equal, a dollar in hand is of more motivational value than a dollar in fringe benefits. Without downgrading or reversing current trends regarding fringe benefits, it is better to permit the individual employee free choice as to spending or investing for additional insurance, retirement income, etc.

Up-to-date compensation plans. Competitive hiring rates and substantial cost of living increases must be recognized and their implications analyzed. There is no magic formula that can be applied indiscriminately. A general approach can be developed, however, for keeping current with the times. Outmoded programs foster dissatisfaction, resentment and loss of confidence in management.

To be fully effective as a motivator, an organization's compensation policy must relate to the individual's contribution to organizational goals and objectives. There are a number of accepted practices which should be used as guidelines.

1. Merit increases should be meaningful. Token increases (less than seven percent for executives) invite feelings and/or remarks such as "you must need it more than I do, keep it".

2. Promotional increases should be given at the time of promotion. Adding responsibility while delaying a salary increase until the completion of a trial period serves to disturb rather than to motivate.

3. Make certain that salary levels of similar departments or divisions within the company are comparable. Failure to keep an eye on this factor will result in capable people scrambling to get out of areas they believe to be of lesser importance to the organization.

4. Relate the individual's salary to his performance as a contributor to the organization at performance meetings between supervisor and subordinate.

5. Maintain written guidelines and policies regarding organizational compensation principles and procedures. Make these available to all supervisory personnel with the understanding that they may be shown to any employee at his request.

6. Maintain and provide statistical data for management so as to insure equity, control and efficient use of funds.

7. Recognize as fiction the idea that salaries are kept secret and that individuals do not compare notes.

There is no panacea for compensation problems nor is there complete applicability and transferability of company or industry plans. Organizations should make every effort to be as innovative as possible in dealing with individual employees. While it is true that government regulations require non-discriminatory application of certain fringe benefits and profit-sharing programs, flexibility for the purpose of increasing individual performance and motivation is extremely important. Where an organization can satisfy individual needs, (e.g. the older employee preferring a greater percentage of deferred income) means should be sought to accomplish this. It is probably true that individual programs involve increased administrative costs. Doesn't the organization gain, however, if these costs are offset by improved performance?

COMMON FALLACIES

The compensation field is unfortunately too often shrouded in secrecy and the result is a great number of fallacious assumptions. Here are a few examples:

Base salary plays a minor role in job satisfaction. Each individual is not motivated by the same factors and money retains great importance for both material value and as a symbol.

Fringe benefits are more important in attracting people than money. A high paying company with marginal fringes will attract many more highly qualified people than a low paying organization with outstanding benefits. Once a base salary meets an individual's needs or expectations, job satisfaction quite often comes from factors such as a participative environment rather than insurance or pension programs.

After a point, money loses its impact. With our income tax structure being what it is, a salary increase, so it is argued, from $75,000 to $100,000 is meaningless. While it may not mean a great deal as a financial increment, motivationally it can be substantially rewarding.

Compensation matters are kept confidential. As it relates to the individual, it should be a matter between supervisor and subordinate. Overall policies, programs, practices and procedures should be common knowledge if there is to be openness, understanding and acceptance.

Compensation is a science. This type of thinking implies easy answers, pat formulas and universal solutions. Developing and implementing plans and programs which can be applied to a large group of employees on an individual basis is an art and a challenge requiring constant attention.

THE FUTURE

We appear to be in a long term inflationary era with the end nowhere in sight. Between 1956 and 1966, starting salaries for non-technical MBA graduates doubled. It is conceivable that starting salaries for bachelor degree holders in 1975 will be in the area of $13,000 per year.

Along with base salary increases, we may see such items as dental insurance, psychiatric services, year long sabbaticals, and the 30 hour work week.

There will probably be much more employee participation in determining work and benefit patterns. It is also fair to assume that the government will exert increasing influence in all areas of compensation.

8

INTERVIEWING

Just as there are definite skills which can be developed to help an individual become a more effective speaker, there are principles and practices which enable a person to become a more effective interviewer. First, increase your ability to understand through listening. Listening in this sense involves a specific means of determining what another individual is really trying to say and giving him an opportunity to fully express himself.

Far from being a tool used primarily by personnel specialists, interviewing skills are essential for the manager who wishes to maintain effective channels of communication; both upward and downward. The manager we are speaking of not only has the ability to give direction but also seeks to obtain the information which is necessary for his decision making.

There are general principles which can be applied to interviewing. Since human beings are endowed with unique capacities and circumstances can be so varied, there is no one pattern or approach which should be adopted *in toto*. Each individual develops his own style which he modifies according to the situation. Principles in this area must be adapted (a) to the interviewer's personality and the approach with which he is most comfortable, and (b) to the specific conditions of the moment.

THE DIRECTIVE INTERVIEW

There are situations where the manager requires certain specific information or is concerned with clarifying a particular problem area. Examples whould be an employment interview or grievance meeting with a union. In either case, certain specific areas must be covered and particular details obtained. Under these circumstances, the interviewer must assume a more direct control of the meeting.

In preparing for an interview of this type, make sure that you define your objectives. What do you wish to accomplish? Do you have as much information as possible concerning the person with whom you are about to talk? In spite of the fact that you are going to structure and direct this interview, try to anticipate and analyze the interviewee's point of view. Examine your .attitudes and try to determine how your goals and objectives will affect those of the interviewee.

In spite of the fact that the interviewer sets the tone and pace of the directive interview, he can still establish and utilize an open atmosphere. This can be accomplished by making the interviewee feel that you want him to exchange his opinions with yours without fear of repercussion. Don't rush things. The interviewee in a successful interview of this kind should be able to relate his own feelings, experiences and values with what is being said. It takes some time, however, for an interviewee to open up and speak freely.

Allow a proper amount of time for the interviewee to answer direct questions. If responses are not clear or appear confused, encourage the individual to clarify his answer. An interrogation session characterized by "machine gun" type questions and answers too often ends in confusion and resentment. If the interviewer can establish a relaxed atmosphere and convey a feeling that encourages the interviewee to express himself, the interviewing process will achieve greater acceptance and succeeding interviews will be able to proceed with less sparring and fewer communications barriers.

A directive interview, as the name implies, is characterized by questions and objectives which are fully controlled by the interviewer. The goals of the interview can be best achieved by careful questioning in a reasonably relaxed atmosphere.

THE NON-DIRECTIVE INTERVIEW

It is a truism that we often do not say what we mean. Fear and confusion restricts and distorts our expression of opinion concerning problems which involve emotions or attitudinal conflicts. The goal of a non-directive interview is to get beyond superficial statements and determine what an individual really feels in a given situation.

This technique is not the easiest for many executives to apply. A successful executive is often a person who "takes charge"—a pragmatic individual who may dominate his department, division or company. After all, this man is paid to achieve results, direct others and to give orders. He is often characterized by his subordinates as someone who wants to get to the point right away and doesn't want to waste time. Problems arise, however, when he becomes so busy giving directions that he forgets or neglects to utilize an ability which certainly played a role in enabling him to rise through the organization— listening.

The non-directive—listening approach can be of great help in dealing with attitudinal or emotional barriers which stand in the way of understanding. The elimination of these obstacles can save a great deal of "wheel spinning" and further enable a group to achieve its objectives more readily through solving or at least bringing to the surface problems which hinder or prevent a sense of personal commitment.

In a non-directive interview a completely permissive atmosphere is established so as to encourage the interviewee to say exactly what he feels. Through a variety of techniques (to be discussed later) the interviewer appears to pass the control of the interview to the interviewee. When the latter feels that the interviewer is really interested in what concerns him, he will open up and bring to the surface what is really bothering him.

The interviewer must not only listen; he must listen with understanding and acceptance. The interviewer need not agree with what is being said. To disagree during the interview, however, generally serves to cut off the flow of information and opinion. We cannot always accept a statement at face value because an individual may not want to say what he means or our perception may cause us to misinterpret. When allowed to expand his remarks, his true feelings may emerge.

Intelligent use of the non-directive approach can result in a mutually beneficial exchange. The subordinate can develop a better understanding of himself, a situation and his relationship to it. The supervisor, in turn, will obtain a better understanding of the individual, the situation and the way his subordinate looks at that situation. A well handled non-directive interview should also give an executive a fairly good gauge of the kind of acceptance his decision or conclusion has been or will be received. Success in this area depends on a desire to understand and a sensitivity to the feelings and attitudes behind the spoken words.

SOME TECHNIQUES

So as to avoid the natural tendency to "take over", special care must be taken to recognize and utilize responses. Some should be avoided while others must be developed.

Two types of responses which should be avoided are:

A. *The Evaluative Response* — In this response, the value judgment of the interviewer (either agreement or disagreement) is evident. e.g. "The army certainly makes a man of you".

B. *The Probing Response* — In this case, the interviewer is narrowing down the area for consideration by the interviewee. When discussing the college experience of an applicant who had indicated some general dissatisfaction with this period of his life, the probing response might be, "you were unhappy with the curriculum at State?"

Responses which are non-directive and show a desire for understanding are neutral in the sense that they encourage the person being interviewed to continue the conversation in his own way. Some of the techniques which encourage this are:

A. Respond by manner — show that you are listening through a nod of the head as well as such comments as "I see" and "uh-huh".

B. When a new piece of information or the expression of an attitude is volunteered, the "tell me more" response will encourage the interviewee to expand further concerning his meaning.

C. Silence — If the interviewer is talking more than 15% of the time, he is not doing, as a general rule, a good job. If the interviewer wants information, he will do well to allow the other person, within reason, to continue talking. This is not meant to allow excessive rambling.

D. The interviewer must interpret meaning. There is always the danger of taking a remark out of context and jumping to a conclusion. As a means of testing what was meant, repeat the closing comment by turning it into a question. If he said, "I have always been interested in retailing", respond with "You have always been interested in retailing?"

E. In order to minimize the possibility of misunderstanding, it is a good idea to summarize frequently to see whether the interviewer understood the interviewee correctly. "As I understand you . . ." is a good preface for these summaries.

SKILLFUL QUESTIONING

Direct questions which require a "yes" or "no" answer or a statistical bit of information should be used as a last resort. Open-ended questions will usually provide the desired information along with amplification on the part of the interviewee.

Employment Interviewing—When interviewing a prospective employee who has recently been graduated from college, one could use an opening such as, "Tell me about yourself. Since 1966 (or whatever year he entered college) what do you feel you have achieved, what have you accomplished; what has been important to you". This gives the applicant a chance to state his own priority of importance. Where the interviewer feels that areas have been omitted, he can direct more specific questions. Even these queries, however, will provide him with greater depth of response if he utilizes open-ended questions. Examples of these would include:

A. "Tell me more about your education in terms of the courses you enjoyed best and least; general level of grades, any activities or sports you participated in and any offices you may have held".

B. "You have held a number of jobs. Tell me about them in terms of your duties and responsibilities, aspects of the job you liked best, those which you enjoyed least, and salary level.

Some guidelines for employment interviewing are:

* Let the interview follow a simple outline.

* Set the candidate at ease.

* Maintain good communications—listen.
* Make a just decision.
* Beware of stereotyping people.
* *Do*
    listen
    avoid interruptions
    find out how he feels about: jobs, people, himself.
* *Don't*
    argue
    reveal your own negative reactions
    give away the "right" answers
    talk about irrelevant things.

APPRAISAL INTERVIEWS

The purpose of this type of interview is to promote more effective working relationships between the supervisor and his subordinate. While rewards or the lack of them—punishment, may appear uppermost in the mind of the interviewee at the time, the direction of the conversation must be related to the effectiveness of the individual; what each (supervisor and subordinate) interprets as the nature of the job and what progress was made towards the achievement of agreed-upon goals. The supervisor should spend at least as much time as the subordinate in preparation for the interview. The subordinate should be asked to prepare for this meeting by appraising his own performance since the last session of this kind and he should be prepared to state his goals and objectives for the period ahead.

Many supervisors begin appraisal interviews by reviewing his subordinate's strong points and then mention weaknesses. This approach is generally correct but the timing must be handled intuitively. If it is stilted the employee will feel that compliments are meaningless and serve only to sugar-coat the criticisms that follow.

The purpose, again, of this interview is to review performance; to identify goals and objectives and to possibly change attitudes if these are hindering satisfactory performance. An outcome of this interview may be a change in working relationships which will maximize the effectness of the supervisor-subordinate team.

If a subordinate disagrees with his supervisor's appraisal and the supervisor treats this disagreement as insubordination, he may never learn why the disagreement exists. He will be in no position, moreover, to effectively combat what is bound to be a deteriorating situation. This is not meant to preclude telling an employee exactly where he stands with his boss. Every effort should be made to get the employee's point of view.

Concentrate on areas of possible improvement related to job functions. Specific examples should be given with suggestions as to what might have been done differently. Suggestions should be constructive; not vague and merely critical.

Towards the end of an appraisal interview, emphasize a job of self-appraisal. Accept the belief that most employees want to improve and take pride in their work. Recognition of effort and productivity is a very important motivator to a valued employee.

9

EFFECTING ORGANIZATIONAL CHANGE

In this century virtually every aspect of our way of living can be characterized in terms of growth. Every area of concern or endeavor; be it business, religion, government, education or recreation has witnessed a phenomenal increase in dollars spent, people involved and areas covered. With this mighty movement has come new approaches and new technology. Production and distribution channels have been radically altered. It is probably correct to note (sadly) that at least two major world wars have served to stimulate these two factors of growth and change.

Our business organizations certainly reflect the changes which were considered necessary to meet the needs and challenges which a growth economy presented: the burgeoning of many giant corporations, wide dispersion of ownership and the emergence of a professional managerial or executive corps.

To a large extent corporate well-being rests on the ability of the organization to adjust, change or modify its structure and approach in relation to shifting product demands, labor markets and production processes. More emphasis, therefore, has been given to long-range planning and the ability of the organization to deliberately introduce and control change to its advantage. Towards this end we have witnessed a strong trend in the direction of decentralization. It is simply unworkable to have all major decisions for a large multi-location organization made by a few men in top management who are located at a central headquarters. For our purposes, we shall concern ourselves with the kind of changes within an organization which reflect fundamental shifts in approaches to maintaining a healthy economic position, i.e. making a profit with decentralization as a primary means and case in point.

"WHY CHANGE?"

In many organizations, reluctance to change is based on the mere fact of the organization's existence. "We must be doing quite a number of things right", so they say, "if we are still in business". The fact that they are operating at much less than capacity or maximum efficiency or profitability is of little importance. The introduction of change is also opposed by many since it often means altering accustomed and comfortable behavior patterns and personal relationships. Finally, and perhaps most importantly, change carries with it no certainty of success. There is always the possibility that change may result in a weaker organization which is less effficient and less profitable. A managerial decision for a given change must be based upon its belief that a change is necessary and a conviction that specific changes will result in a strengthened organization.

Other Factors

In order to implement change, people must be taught and motivated to accomplish their work in a different manner. Learning new skills is generally an operating factor in accomplishing change. Since learning involves effort and most people find it easier to continue doing things as they have done them, competent instructors must be provided to impart the necessary knowledge and technical skills.

In any organization, people will strive to develop and maintain personal relationships which are satisfying to them. Anyone attempting change which will markedly affect these structurings should be aware of a great deal of resistance on the part of those who view the status quo as satisfying and protective.

Perhaps the dimensions of the problems of a major change within any organization can be seen best if we recognize the diversity of concerns which may exert an influence:

1. The history of the organization
2. Its relationship with government, unions, the community in which it is located and the industry of which it is a part
3. The economic environment
4. Psychological aspects which include elements of learning theory—how behavior patterns and skills are acquired, irrational or unconscious factors which influence behavior such as stress and anxiety, and an understanding of how small groups function—their effect on individual behavior, as well as their influence on the larger organization—group dynamics.

RECOGNITION

Most companies provide for enough feedback of information in enough areas to recognize the existence of weakness in any phase of their operations. Awareness of a weakness, however, and the specific knowledge of what has gone wrong and what to do about it are often two completely separate items. Problem areas may be viewed one way by production people, another by those in sales and in a completely different light by those in the controller's office. In fact, weaknesses may be the result of a number of factors. These might include: inadequacy of the people involved, the method of operation, or the organizational structure.

CLIMATE

In attempting to institute change, one must be aware of the informal and actual relationship as opposed to a strict organization chart analysis. A number of positions which in the company handbook are listed as top management may be held by individuals whose influence in the organization may be relatively minor. These types of situations exist at virtually every level of an organization.

Although it may be vociferously denied, every organization to some extent bears a resemblance to a political party in the sense that both formal and informal power groupings with leaders and supporters operate and are recognized as such.

Two extreme economic factors are likely to promote inertia and hinder the chances for major changes. In times of a boom economy and high profits, many companies don't want to bother with the difficulties of going through a change. In times of depression, on the other hand, all energies are devoted to staying alive and substantial reform within the organization is considered too much of a luxury to be undertaken.

The two conditions which are most likely to provide a receptive attitude towards change are:

1. A period of great expansion when management realizes that the old structure is no longer meaningful with current spans of control no longer operative; and

2. When a company feels that its competitive position is in jeopardy with continued decline as the long range forecast—the Ford Motor Company at the end of World War II is a case in point.

COMMITMENT

Top management's commitment to the need for change is crucial for success. In times of good profits and reasonable growth, many companies prefer security and stability to the lure of still higher profits. There is a direct relationship between support for an aggressive program of action and the size of the gap between management's level of expectation and the company's current level of operations. A word of caution—there are executives who seem to prefer change for change's sake. This is the kind of person who if he were in the army, enjoyed "shaking up the troops". In civilian life he continues the same pattern. In many cases, his associates have learned to cope with this type of behavior. Their reaction may consist of sitting tight when the periodic storms occur and just wait for the problem to blow over. This attitude obviously diminishes commitment.

Cost Factor—Commitment must include a willingness to bear the costs of change. No management can be expected to give a blank check to anyone. Concrete recommendations as to the cost of change and the risks involved will allay many fears. Changes, however, are seldom accomplished overnight. The transition period, with its uncertainties will invariably result in a greater cost of getting the work done. Those who are responsible for guiding these programs would do well to indicate most clearly what improvements will accrue to the company as a result of the proposed changes.

Outside Consultants—As a means of coping with uncertainty, particularly where a proposed change has widespread consequences, an outside consultant can be used to advantage. Assuming they have the required technical knowledge, they can provide an element of objectivity since they have nothing to gain by either acceptance or rejection of a program.

Provision for phasing—The chances for success can be further strengthened by attacking those areas where changes can quickly yield substantial results through improved operations. Generally, planned programs of change deal with the less difficult problems first in order to allow the reorganization to capitalize on both momentum and acceptance.

IMPLEMENTATION

A planned program for change must indicate to all concerned what changes in terms of methods of operation and behavior are expected of them.

Negative motivation (punishment) usually fails as a means of improving or changing an individual's performance. Positive rewards have proven to be far more successful in this regard. Oftentimes a powerful incentive is the recognition that change will allow an individual to do more responsible and meaningful work.

Recognizing that a period of change is one that carries with it a great deal of tension and turmoil, top management must make every effort to support people so as to minimize anxieties.

FEEDBACK

Since there is always a great danger that actual change may be more fiction than truth, top management must ascertain whether people are actually doing their jobs as they are supposed to under the new program. In a similar vein, actual results can be measured against anticipated results. Finally, management must also be alert to the necessity of revising time schedules for phasing in a new program.

10

THE FUTURE

In an era of population explosions, the emergence of new nations, and the recognition of new vistas in both technology and utilization of our human resources, it would be extremely difficult to pinpoint the direction business organizations will take in the future. It does seem fairly safe, however, to anticipate a number of trends which the personnel manager will have to contend with:

1. Increased governmental regulation—in the areas of compensation, pensions and even employment. We may not be too far away from guaranteed annual incomes, pension funds which an employee may take with him to another firm and government employment exchanges.

2. Increased complexity of operations—greater application of the computer to personnel activities; larger organizations which require a higher order of ability to manage without losing sight of the individual employee.

3. A chronic shortage of manpower in terms of both management talent and skilled labor.

4. A need to make work more meaningful and productive—As basic needs are increasingly satisfied through social legislation; as the work week declines and as members of the "affluent society" become less money oriented, business organizations must devise new approaches to stimulate both creativity and productivity—the development of new and better solutions to current and long range problems and the effective application of current methods and techniques.

These are some of the problems that organizations and personnel managers will deal with. They are challenging and complex and panaceas are non-existent. Personnel Management offers the multi-hued fabric of nuances to those who prefer this type of complexity.

SUGGESTED READINGS

Argyris, C. *Personality and Organization*. New York: Harper & Row, 1957.

Blake, R. and Mouton, J. *The Managerial Grid*. Houston: Gulf, 1964.

Blood, J. *The Personnel Job In A Changing World*. New York: AMA, 1964.

Drucker, Peter. *The Practice of Management*. New York: Harper, 1954.

Drucker, Peter. *The Effective Executive*. New York: Harper & Row, 1967.

Fear, R. *The Evaluation Interview*. New York: McGraw-Hill, 1958.

Gellerman, S. *Motivation and Productivity*. New York: AMA, 1963.

Hinrichs, J. *High-Talent Personnel*. New York: AMA, 1966.

Hoslett, S. *Human Factors in Management*. New York: Harper, 1946.

Likert, R. *New Patterns of Management*. New York: McGraw-Hill, 1961.

Mahler, W. "Systems Approach to Managing by Objectives". *Systems and Procedures Journal*, New York; September, 1965.

Marrow, A. *Behind the Executive Mask*. New York: AMA, 1964.

McGregor, D. *The Human Side of Enterprise*. New York: McGraw-Hill, 1960.

McGregor, D. *The Professional Manager*. New York: McGraw-Hill, 1967.

Nadler, G. *Work Simplification*. New York: McGraw-Hill, 1957.

Rowland, V. *Improving Managerial Performance*. New York: Harper, 1958.

Sayles, L. and Strauss, G. *The Human Problems of Management*. New Jersey: Prentice-Hall, 1960.

Schleh, E.C. *Management by Results: The Dynamics of Profitable Management.* New York: McGraw-Hill, 1961.

Sibson, R. *Wages and Salaries.* New York: AMA, 1967.

Symposium *What's Wrong With Work?* New York: NAM, 1967.

Vroom, V. *Work and Motivation.* New York: Wiley, 1964.

INDEX

Titles in the
BUSINESS ALMANAC SERIES

Additional copies or titles may be ordered from:
Department BAS, Oceana Publications, Inc.
Dobbs Ferry, New York 10522

What You Should Know About